come from

come from

poems

---

janan alexandra

Foreword by Ross Gay

NEW POETS OF AMERICA SERIES NO. 56

BOA EDITIONS, LTD. * ROCHESTER, NY * 2025

Copyright © 2025 by janan alexandra
Foreword copyright © 2025 by Ross Gay

All rights reserved
Manufactured in the United States of America

First Edition
23 24 25 26 7 6 5 4 3 2 1

For information about permission to reuse any material from this book, please contact The Permissions Company at www.permissionscompany.com or e-mail permdude@gmail.com.

Publications by BOA Editions, Ltd.—a not-for-profit corporation under section 501 (c) (3) of the United States Internal Revenue Code—are made possible with funds from a variety of sources, including public funds from the Literature Program of the National Endowment for the Arts; the New York State Council on the Arts, a state agency; and the County of Monroe, NY. Private funding sources include the Max and Marian Farash Charitable Foundation; the Mary S. Mulligan Charitable Trust; the Rochester Area Community Foundation; the Ames Amzalak Memorial Trust in memory of Henry Ames, Semon Amzalak, and Dan Amzalak; and contributions from many individuals nationwide. See Colophon on page 115 for special individual acknowledgments.

Cover Artwork: "Crossing Paths," circa 1974, oil on canvas by Amine El Bacha, courtesy of the Amine El Bacha Foundation, © 2024 Amine El Bacha. Used with permission.
Cover art and Design: Sandy Knight
Interior Design and Composition: Isabella Madeira
BOA Logo: Mirko

BOA Editions books are available electronically through BookShare, an online distributor offering Large-Print, Braille, Multimedia Audio Book, and Dyslexic formats, as well as through e-readers that feature text to speech capabilities.

Cataloging-in-Publication Data is available from the Library of Congress.

BOA Editions, Ltd.
250 North Goodman Street, Suite 306
Rochester, NY 14607
www.boaeditions.org
A. Poulin, Jr., Founder (1938-1996)

Contents

Foreword   11

I.

Invocation   15
Heritage Language   17
Origin Story   18
Transit   23
Homecoming, ft. Free Dates   24
When I Wake   26
Strays   27
On Form & Matter   28
How the Dream Ends   29

II.

Notes on Touch   33
Now that You're Gone   34
Requiem for the Blue-Headed Morning   36
Ode to Crying at the Supermarket   38
Litany of the Right Hand   40
On the Last Day   42
Just Had to Tell Somebody   43
Ars Poetica   45
Affirmation   46

III.

Standing at the Window   51
Dream, or Poem to the Tongue   53

Return (the wish)   54
Return (the retelling)   55
Inert for Days the Living Shadows   56
On Sisterhood   57
Come From   58
Return (the etymologies)   59
Learning to Write in Arabic   60

IV.

parable of the aleph   65
parable of the three sisters   66
parable of the three cousins   69
parable of broken bones   72
parable of the field   74
parable of thanks   77
parable of sound & grammar   79
parable of sharing   81
parable of the eye in the throat   83
parable as ars poetica   85
parable of water & mothers   87
parable of the monostich   90

IV.

Arab American Syntax   93

Notes   101
Acknowledgments   105
About the Author   111
Colophon   115

The house is past.

—Adorno

Foreword

If I were lucky enough to introduce you to janan alexandra's marvelous first book, *come from*, by which I really mean if I were to tell you about it what I love, by which I mean begin to tell you about it what I love, I might start with feeling, how the poems themselves feel yes—recklessly, holleringly, precisely—but also how much in the poems there is to feel, to touch; how thick with the palpable world, how in it they are, and of it, how rich with land and people, with elderberries and ankles and eyes and ferns and saplings and oarlocks and cornflowers and hands and throats and tongues and the plush ears of donkeys and the dreams of bats; and then I might say something about how they see, how they look at and attend, something about their attention and regard, how close they seem to get, to be, how cheek to cheek, how heart to heart; and I might wonder about attention, about regard as a kind of music that plays us, or sings us; I might wonder with you about how the attention in these poems, the closeness, is a kind of love; and how the closeness, the regard, seems to animate the language and light up the diction, which is a curious diction, a diction of curiosity; how the noticing, how the closeness, the curiosity makes the music I'm saying; how the unknowing is a kind of music I'm saying and how the feeling and the closeness too make a kind of music; how they feel these poems I love; and how these poems put their hands before them through the dark, how they learn, how they change, how they try again, and again; and how unfixed they are, and unfixing; and how lost they are, and reaching; how in love they are, sturdy in it, rugged and pervious; how they belt their love, and how they sorrow their love too; how they sorrow I love, and how they do not specimen their sorrow nor moat it nor covet it, but seem to wonder, to *know*, it is something like your sorrow this sorrow, to be unmoored, do be ungrounded, this reaching we do through the dark, and I cannot explain it, but the poems, not only their sorrow, but their glee and their wonder and their tumult and their goddamn too, they somehow open their arms to us and bring us in, they set a place and say you can be here, you can rest here, right where you can hear the birds singing, the loves, the roots reaching as they are through the dark, toward us, always, I love these poems how they make welcome.

—Ross Gay

I.

Invocation

i call my mother
to ask her the word

knowing there's
no english

for this which
has a name

in arabic: (   )

among all she did
& didn't teach us

we learned to scour
dishes with cold water

& coffee grounds,
trick for losing

the stink left
by a broken yolk.

i ask for this word
i've forgotten,

to carry its flap
in my mouth,

small utterance
of a loss i practice

& repeat, hope
to repair. tell me,

when i can
no longer call,

what else will
have no name?

Heritage Language

when we came to america
an archive locked
baby teeth
fastened
around a silence
our lips made
hanging circles in the air
a shapely absence

she kept records
in her jewelry box:
a clutch of hair
wrapped in paper
the small sukuun
little roundness
keyhole, doorway
we peered through

Origin Story

١

we are whirling
    through Beirut
the city i visit most
    often in my sleep
i take this to mean
    i am making
my best effort
    to dream in Arabic
where the air
    is rich with orange
flowers & thyme
    & we draw
back our lips
    to speak

٢

in the so-called city
that never sleeps
i tight rope along
the edge of cobble-
stones bathed in light
& last week's trash

i dream by nose
the heavy stench
of garbage rotting
into the sweet
fresh ka'ak
golden purses
who ride the air
like wooden boats

in my ear a moped
twists & guzzles
the pitted road
spitting gravel under
the too slow heel
of somebody's foot

٣

somebody's foot grazes
mine & i find a boy there

gazing in at me through
the small eyehole of my sleep

i have forgotten his name
until my mother reminds me

It's Hani   there in a teal t-shirt
black irises flowering from his eyes

*

one summer afternoon
with Hani   we swam & played

licking ice pops   sticky lipped
on the stone apartment steps

our knees slapping open
to greet the turquoise sea

we floated weightless
our bodies fanning starfish

*

later that day i learned my first
lesson on the dangers of touch

& electricity in Beirut—
though i had been warned

i yanked open the refrigerator door—
a sudden shock of light jolting

my arm from inside   a blade
zigzagging hot through my bones

ع

when asked about his time in Beirut,
Mahmoud Darwish said:

"Poetry requires a stable temperature, around twenty degrees Celsius!
Ice and very hot weather kill poetry, and Beirut was boiling.
Boiling with feelings and visions. Beirut was a land of perplexity."

ه

dear land of perplexity
i think i understand
what the Poet means

everyone always clicks
their teeth soberly & says
the situation is very bad

& in the same breath
a phoenix appears
in love with living

who   for the sake
of a new beginning
will burn itself alive

٦

dear secret stairways
painted brightly   sing song
greetings i know & do not know

dear orange juice held
in squat paper pouches
sleeves of Nescafé

dear mushroom shop
candy stall   your lengths
& ribbons of sweets

unrolling like the tongue's
lottery tickets   dotted
with pink & blue treats

i sling my arm around
your balconies at night
catch myself falling

through the house
with windows blown
out   face agape

٧

as the story goes
we once lived
in a beige house:

two parents
two sisters
one black cat

two turtles
who left

& never
came back.

Transit

i touch my face to the oval window,
peering out from my seat in the sky.
i am small, tinier even than a housefly
riding the edge of a cloud. at the bottom
of my sight cars hug the winding roads.
city buses lurch & sway, packed with the people
of the world. a freight train cuts soundlessly
through sepia fields & i feel my fly's forehead
wrinkle at the hard lacework of highways
hammered & poured, twisting around earth.
how like ants we are, plotting our routes
for food, for our children, for industry.
drilling through hills of sand & clay to get where
we want to go. how still & silent the stretch
of land from up here. no tunnel torn through
the valley's waist. nor forest fired or felled,
no oil rig nor pumpjack. nothing to extract
save my eye, wanting not to miss any life
under the mist. i press further into the glass.
i know the trees speak 30,000 feet below,
leaf floor clicking with the errands of insects.

Homecoming, ft. Free Dates

Around the corner the ground is covered
with dates, sunlight drizzled like honey
atop clusters of warm wrinkled fruit.

Have you ever seen a date? Really studied one?
Be honest. We called them cockroaches
as children, a little ashamed of the absence

of Oreos & Twizzlers & whatever else
the mostly American kids washed down
with Capri-Sun after school. Let me explain:

the date is chewy with decay & the nutty sweet
of slow cooked sugar. The date is like god's
toffee, god's granny's homemade caramel.

You can tell, I am reformed. Returned.
Assimilation lasts only so long before
we become our mothers & conjure a way

back to the homeland, which exists mostly
on our tongues, because mostly the home
is long gone, rubbled or razed to the ground,

but hey, here it is now as my tongue tongues
the pit of this. I can't believe my luck: free
dates! I gather what I can carry in my hands

as the rooster wails his small & holy song,
repeating *it is day! it is day!* & the adhan
echoes across the dusty mountaintops.

I think of my mother opening the doors
of the namliyeh she painted to match the sky,
her fingers deep in dried figs, dates, almonds

& walnuts. *In our part of the world*, she'd say, *this is dessert.* Part of the world where I stand now, a little alone, a stranger a little less.

When I Wake

my heels hang
    like two bats

deep in a dream
    of field mice.

today there are
    no black hours,

& the one beside me
    digs my limbs

out from under
    the quilt, presses

low into my bones
    'til i'm restrung

& standing. i return
    this mercy later,

gathering oranges
    in the worn belly

of my shirt like
    my father before me,

wringing out the juice
    after rolling the fruit

between my palms
    to loosen the rind.

Strays

each morning i find the same marbled calico
asleep against our water heater, her scrap
of gooey-eyed kittens batting flies beneath
the solar panel. like them i follow the sun,
moving from this place to that. but even here,
home of the lemon, winter seeps through
the walls. the cats seek heat where they can,
body to body on the engine-warm hoods of cars,
or in flowerpots stuffed with leaves. for now
we linger late in pools of soleil, Fairuz singing
while coffee swells on the stovetop. the days
are long & lined with hours. i swing open
the shutters as if to keep the light.

On Form & Matter

i was folding somebody else's sheets at the communal laundry line. the communal laundry line was in the gardens. in the gardens the sheets hung brightly purple & green. they were fitted sheets. queen or full size. their paisley pattern was called "american swirl." from here i thought the sheets were a field of violets. i thought the field swung from the line, clumps of purple flowers forming along a thin crust of grass. i coveted them. the grassy sheets. the violet field rippling on the line. i thought & said out loud *you know what i love is bedding*. & i wondered. what is a reasonable thing to love? A reasonable number of sheets to have? below, my heart shrugged. bored with reason. above, my head ventured, *two?* the two of us bat the freckled egg of wonder back & forth until we agree: two cotton sets of sheets plus one flannel batch for the cold. & so. i returned to my task. my task which was slowly gathering someone else's bedding. like wrapping a gift. like it was someone's birthday. which it must have been. as it must be now. i smoothed the cloth & pulled out the creases, tucked each frowning corner into the other. you know how fitted sheets are. this is one way to fold them so that the edges might meet. tante cécile taught me years ago. & so. for each matter a form. a from. what is reasonable? asks the mind once more. this i love & so what, the heart repeats.

How the Dream Ends

On the road to Karpaz you pass a field of wild donkeys
grazing in the last low hour of sun.
Once, you fed a donkey carrots loosed from a sack
in the stone cellar. You let the donkey's lips search the tender flat
of your palm, nibbling for the carrot & salt.
This was your first donkey. You saw then
that donkey teeth were beautiful teeth, pushing open
like shutters. Months later, a farmer old enough to be your father
would teach you to pull back the donkey's ear,
lower your face into the crease & breathe in.
He would say *meilleure du monde, l'odeur derrière l'oreille de l'âne*.
You sat together, passing a cigarette back & forth
while you watched the donkeys sleep upright on all fours,
their brows pressed to the wooden fence post.
In those days your head was bare, a fuchsia scarf trailing
from your neck like bougainvillea. Your shoulders broadened
as you strapped your work boots to your back.
Little pack mule climbing the hills & eating
from the ferns. Walking with your life & load.
Digging for the flask of tea & day-old bread,
you scanned the gorge for a place to rest.
It was you, back then. Still is. Sometimes
the morning starts with a chariot of suns
charging the cover of night inside your chest.
You bolt upright, weeping at the edge of the bed.
Sometimes you're at the end of the dream
undone. The distance runner in your heart spits
& sprints toward the finish, arms pumping,
feet kicking up clouds of dust. The path disappears.
The dream dissolves. But on the road to Karpaz,
memory surfaces in shiny scraps of trash & glass
washing up in the drift. Bottle caps, lighters,
old beer cans. You squat in the bleached sand
searching for the smallest shells & now you are
pulling leeks from the ground again. Now a child

curled in a field of cobalt corn flowers, crying a little
for the foal who left & never returned. Were you that animal, too?
Hungry & far from your mother, crossing the red dirt alone.

II.

Notes on Touch

Sure, life also includes staring at ice flakes
in thawing compost, sweeping debris.

When I push the broom across the floor,
dust springs alive. I am here as you are there

somewhere. Together we miss the touch
of the world, beautiful & awful. But still,

the birds aren't closed today. The birds
don't stop their happy racket. This robin

just flopped down in the grass by me.
When I speak, her head twitches. I wish

she would climb into my hand, I wish it
silently in my heart. It is invisible but near

constant, the urge to touch. To make
& learn by feel. To be known by hand—

what else is there! Some want sex twice a day
& others have lost all desire. Regardless,

the walk across the yard is still the walk across
the yard. Everything keeps on, lives & squeaks.

I scrub the mudroom & find moss dotting
the stone steps like stubble. I love it as I love

every face as a face I might press my cheek to.

Now that You're Gone

I'm back
    to riding my bike
alone. I glide by shorn
    grass & slip
into the blue field with-
    out you. I confess
everything we did
    to the horses.
Why should they care?
    The russet mare
flicks her tail, pissing
    while she chews
a clump of cud.

    I leave her
& head for the red
    bridge we sped
across, our fingers
    flushed with touch.
Once, as night settled
    the field, we lay
in the hush of bare trees.
    I pass the ruins
of the old barn & pedal
    harder, locking eyes
with the gravel path.

    When I arrive
at the water's edge
    I take my time.
A grey heron dips
    one leg in & out
of the pond. I lower
    my right foot into
the water, then

>   my left. My ankles
> flocked with wind,
>   two river rocks
> you once turned over
>   in your hands.

Requiem for the Blue-Headed Morning

the devil's in my neck
　　　—Thomas Lux

If I am good, I cannot tell you
who or what I love, but if I am here,
I can say needle-sharp & knotted,
wedged like a pebble in the slat.
The milk's gone off. Here comes the rancid oil
& the rat. I have no bolt of silk, no sugar
in my tin. Paint's dried up; glue is too.
Can't fill the cracks or nix the blue.
If I am asking, it's how to love
what lines my palms. Unclench my teeth.
Break into a smile & relax the bit.
See, when I sing, I lose my breath.
The music doesn't hover or stretch.
Velvet's all wet. Shirt must've shrunk.
Colors bled. Snag & skid. Death got my head.
I gnaw each nail to the pig-pink quick.
But say, for the sake, I sit on my hands.
Count every exhale like my father passing
prayer beads between his finger & thumb.
Say I stay on the downbeat. Release what was
never to be held or kept. Say I touch
the same raw skin 'til finally I say fuck it,
lengthen my gaze past the balding lawn,
offer my eye to the walnut tree who
just now bloomed with six cherry-red wings,
six bright hands waving from the twig
& right below, a pair of squirrels who chase
tails & forget their bulk of nuts, which
in a way makes a gift of what is lost,
a secret meal for some stranger or kin
with a fellow hunger & wisp-thin tongue.
Say this is how to get past the speck of I,

say we are dear, our own dear g, oh g-o-d,
temple of morning light & devil made
blue-in-the-brain. Go live like the critter
who digs every day. Bury the mirror & blade.

Ode to Crying at the Supermarket

The occasion for this bout of tears,
who can remember? But praise anyway

the weeper whose eyes are two salt lakes
filling with cans of soup in aisle 9,

you who waded into Kroger hungry
& listless, wondering Who in the deli

might take a weeper home for dinner
or tuck Who Weeps into a freshly made

bed. Bless the sad men stooping inside
your chest, chain-smoking & spitting

as they toss their sorrow up your throat,
which is rough as the pit in a dark sweet

plum, like this one here called *purple heart*,
whose flesh will ripen right before death.

You know what they say: once a weeper
always a weeper. So what. Weep away

& weigh the rice, wipe your chin, scoot
along the waxed floor trying to add up

your money & remember a time of love
in the grocery store. Somewhere your arm

exists, threaded through hers, steering
the cart together, chariot piled with veggies

& a week of afternoon snacks. Your baby
hands, suddenly two glad animals, two geese

flapping & honking above the conveyor
belt, packing bouquets of greens, lining

each bag with what's heaviest at the base,
loosely draping what's light over the rest.

Litany of the Right Hand

I have held the cat's velvet paw each night
while you sleep. Studied the engine

of her purring against your chest. This sound
has held your rest. In December, I held your sister's

slippered feet, kneading my thumb into her heels,
rubbing the bony root of each toe.

I have held off her fury, it has chased & pinned
you to the ground, held you up, crouched on the curb

in the shadow of a black Oldsmobile. I have
felt the curb's gravel teeth. I have held your mother's

fingers lightly as the furred stems of poppies,
I have curled silent by your hip while you marvel

at these flowers who unfurl orange each year.
Their papier-mâché petals, delicate & crushable.

How the wind might make them torn. Hold them
torn. I have held the tear in your father's neck.

I am holding it now while you speak to him
through the phone. He laughs when you say

the cat drools into her brush. I love how you
hold your father's laughter. It is warm & tired.

You are holding it now. You have leaked & oozed
with laughter. You have wept all day. Your mother

has said *isn't it a bit much?* I have felt your chest
heave. You have sunk the apple of your chin

into me. I have held your head. Yes, I have said
to you each time, touching my face to yours.

On the Last Day

we grate lemon zest into yolks
cracked cold from the fridge,
dip our fingers in cake flour
& fold the yielding yellow dough.

when it's time to say bismillah
& heave her suitcase into the trunk,
taking the terminally gray road
to the airport, we've filled tins

with enough treats to last a week,
two if i ration. still, we have no time
at the gate, cars crowding the curb,
security swatting at us & barking

into their megaphones. inside my throat
the fine needles of an artichoke heart
start to open. i miss her even as we face
each other, knowing what i know

& cannot yet know, coming home
motherless to a house that is lonely
for her jasmine & rose, one strand
of her hair curled upon my pillow.

Just Had to Tell Somebody

the sun's come around & the people
of the sun too, pouring into the streets

like a procession of tambourines.
just thought you'd want to know.

i roll heel to toe through the city,
walhamdulillah springing from my tongue

with more oomph than cherry pits picked clean.
i'm toothy as the boy blowing bubbles

on the corniche, one oblong globe after
another wobbling like foals from the gentle *O*

of his lips. praise be to both what is born
& vanishes midair, atom to atom.

for the first time since we buried you
i turn up my sleeves, unlatch the shutters

like i'm slowly undressing the house.
after you died i became forgetful of the body

in my sorrow, or the sorrow in my body,
neglected to stroke the underarm's cornsilk,

failed to comb the trail of thistles sprouting
along my inner thigh. what's that?

bare ankles & knees? are you kidding,
skin's been on strike. just had to say

miss you. think of you. the alley cats
are all pregnant again, lined up like proud

gods on the garden wall. their eyes are sealed
with light while they wait for what lives &

even the stones oil their faces to gleaming.

Ars Poetica

crows slink by. as shadows in periphery.
their flight a brief ink in the sky. wing swish
like the rustle of clean sheets. our feet fuss
under the quilt 'til we fall asleep. fall in dreams
of houses & water & skin. such is wind. comes
billowing in. thuds the shutters. sweeps my head.
suddens my wonder: how to write 14 true lines.
unlikely sonneteer, i can't stop once i start.
half a page of circumlocuting but i've only
begun to begin. reset the clock & the next line
barges in. is a barge. huge with diffuse cargo.
listen. at this rate, the end could never come.
after all. what would it be? small & round
enough to palm. speechless as a stone.

Affirmation

an armful of light-soaked hay in the driveway. the cool water of the gravel pit where we can swim on our lunch breaks, naked & for free. the kid, probably around seven or eight at the register behind the counter at pili's who really had to pee, a few of us in line waiting to pay for our groceries, all of us cheering her on—go pee, we can wait! the braille of every tree I've leaned into & tried to read, each summer of bug bites that swell to form whole continents on my thighs, maiming my skin, even the insufferable mosquitoes, I wouldn't give them up if it meant losing the world, walking down decatur street, riding the train, watching the painters shift & balance on the scaffolding, suspended from thick ropes, one on each side of the platform, lowering & raising themselves to the squeaking wheels of the rickety pulley, muraling the long brick wall, every stranger I've locked eyes with on the street, every time we agree, nonverbally, to look up, find each other & offer a slight smile, or, god forbid, say hello, I love even that flight attendant who barked at me when I asked for one of each complimentary snack, flying from maine to texas, a long day in the air, my legs heavy & numb, pins & needles down to my toes, nose dry & so I longed to be fed & hoped for a dose of both the sweet & the savory & this lady, stewardess of the sky, looked at me so disdainfully my ears flushed with shame (yes, I cried), but I love the bustle of the world even when it comes in sharp, maybe especially then, knowing the hurt that hurt makes, I love the thready trails & air clean as dirt, the rocks I've pocketed only to return them to the ground soon after, every river where I've freed my feet from their packet of sock & lace, rinsed them or let them wade me into water up to my bony wingtips, I love the busy throngs, the subway singers, the romanian street band, the accordionist under the yellow archway, I love the children everywhere stuffed into coats like puffed marshmallows, their cheeks windburned & chapped, snot caked around their noses like a winter creek, I love to recall that I once rode a motorcycle slowly through winding hills near toulouse, took buses from village to village, got lost & kept walking, touched the same sand as a pod of elephant seals, held their molting skin, once slept in the open mouth of a pipe under the highway, pedaling up & around each hairpin twist of coast, I love the voices of others, the small tasks between strangers, the flirting, the roofers, the chats in the backs of cabs, human hands, the women at the post office clicking their nails, the bank tellers who count money like they're shuffling a deck of cards, fanning the cash between their fingers & flipping each bill with strong square thumbs, the bus drivers wearing gloves for gripping the wheel on each wide turn, the groaning engine that won't ever die, I love the world & its magical acts—snow & triple rainbows, for example—its afternoon naps, its bread, its centuries of wood & blood & bone, I love the fact of gazelles, the old-growth forest & thunderhead cloud, I care about the mess, the osprey nest, the rogue strips of wildflowers that return each year to the meridian between two highways, the bucks grazing too close to the road where they are often left after slaughter, I love the fog & foghorn calling to the boats, the hungry green flies who bite in the sand, the sea roses & their tough horns, the elderberry branches weighing with violet medicine, the old school buildings, I love the ruins, the rain, the cornfields past the dike, the word sassafras, the mothers nursing, the baskets of blankets & diapers, the city cats, the strays, the strain, oh floating world, cell in space, life moving, caring for what lives, living for what cares & moves in us, oh each brief company.

III.

Standing at the Window

When I don't know where to go
I stand at the window & wait.

Each day brings its events:
the high school marching band

bursting into brass circumstance
on the street. A sudden eruption

of pigeons from the olive tree's
shaggy branch. Or stillness:

a stack of terracotta tiles left
for rain by an empty shopping cart

next door. Wait long enough
& a story will take you into its arms:

our neighbor, for instance, who appears
in the garden throughout the day,

rearranging her wash to keep up
with the sun's rotations. Even from

my post upstairs, I hear the sigh spill
from her as she adjusts clothespins,

mouth drawn tight as a coin purse.
She performs this ritual reliably,

trudging across the yard five or six
times a day in cream pink socks

& high-heeled sandals. Sometimes
she stands there for long minutes,

like I do at the sill. Once, I watched
her eyes narrow at the family

of cats living on top of the shed
between us. Slowly she unwound

her garden hose, cursing & spraying
them away with water. Since then,

I do my part to avenge them. Each night,
after my neighbor draws her curtains,

I stand in the wide open window
kissing the air until, one by one,

the cats appear, mama first, a deep
black star puckered where her left eye

used to be, three spotted kittens
scrambling up at her side.

Then, the event of the day: aiming
for the shed, I fling boiled chicken

from my window, slippery hunks
of meat sailing down to reach them.

Dream, or Poem to the Tongue

Gathered around the sudur with a long cloth scroll,
an Arabic newspaper embroidered in red & gold.

& in each thread a kind of time & in each time
a pair of hands clasped on the marble table

hauled from country to country. You too
will make a life of hauling things: books,

your father's carpets once crushed in a flimsy
trunk, now slung over a banister in Indiana,

a century of dust lifting off the loom work.
You too have entered what was only half given.

Inheritance is a field of dispersal. It's alright.
You will spend your life stitching the flaps.

When you dream of windpipes restless & dry
as your sleep, your mother will still be your mother.

You have saved her voice in the telephone & held
this in your hands like the wide blue & white eyes

of her favorite mug. So these are your hands
& this will be your tongue. You too will sing

from the gut, in a language that knows the thickness
of blood, knows how to say & how to say you bury me—

Return
the wish

slowly the notion
of going back slid
away like a name
disappearing

in the dirt
wiped clean
by the wind

gone but for
the sweets my father
brought home in crinkling
golden wrappers

my lips clicking open
for the tart & chewy
amardeen, creamy

squares of nougat
perfumed with rose water
& pistachio,

lump of sugar
i hold like a wish-
bone piercing my cheek

Return
   the retelling

Last night with your mother & father. A kind of family house,
a notion of home. There with your one grandmother who had
strong calves & sleek black stockings stretching across her ankles
which were like stones she loved. Bless her wrists' blue-green
rivers & her teeth & lips that studied poems. Bless your father
who cried & cried in his chair, which in French would mean
in his flesh. His face was smooth as new fruit, eyes like honey
thickly bright. A liquid strange & low pooled in your father's throat
but this time it was not blood & so in his chair he rocked & in his
way became brave & soft. He made a sound of wooden hooves
on the wooden floor & the thousand hands of time were thus
measured in hooves & the rocking of chairs. & here your father's
neck grown silken with grass & what was broken of the skin
had been softly resewn & here was now meant to last & last.

Inert for Days the Living Shadows

have returned, stretching their arms & legs,
sending long dark strokes across new shoots

in the green sheath. Even the drooped ears
of the night blooming cereus are lifting & alert,

reaching up to meet all the fresh light laying like clean
skin around the house. Light who touches doorways,

turns to dappled amber the wooden floorboards
& steam trunk, warming the plump orange

armchair dressed in my Sitto's wool blanket,
which she stitched at one time, threading the bent

branches of her fingers through skeins of yarn,
there in her front room by the sliding glass door,

where the sun gushed in to polish her shepherd's
hook, her granny squares with their black frames

& buttercup hearts, which even now, unraveling,
have kept the blood in my feet, more or less,

three winters long. This cover draped like a hand
on my lap. How her hand would stroke & smooth

the cushions while she pursed her lips, eyes damp
behind her glasses. I think of her now as daylight

strides in, strobing the dust so electric it glitters
in the air like the tiny grandchildren of rain.

On Sisterhood

since we last spoke
i have seen the corpse

of a wolf spider coiled
in the windowsill,

her legs a tangle
of yarn. many nights

i watched her crawl
back & forth

in the thin corridor
between screen & pane,

searching for an opening
though she found none,

checking for a tear
in the flywire, feeling

how near the star-dark air,
imagining the round Oh

of a space through which
to fit her body & slip free.

Come From

if we do not speak
in the night   in the kitchen
here leaning over the starry counter
like two hunched sunflowers

if we do not stand   stooped
like this   picking at cold lasagna
which is neither the food
of your country   nor my own
how will we carry this tin pail
sloshing   with the question

can you imagine walking
into a softly lit room
in the world & feeling
hereiam, homewithallofyou?

to be known in the arithmetic
of belonging   we follow
an order   of operations

we do the math
    enough   & not enough.
what are you   really really?
    from from?

really we are   the field
in each other's eyes

we hope   to die surrounded
by our own languages—
even those we cannot speak

Return
 the etymologies

exile might mean no country but it's also the place we live now

country could be a loneliness or a grassy hill with straw & horses

home could be a missing tongue when asked *where are you from?*

land might mean to arrive, or receive, or, green-gold meadow

return could mean to give back or come back or go back
                                          or to turn once more

Learning to Write in Arabic

(i) *sheen*

i wake with the shape
of the ش in my right hand

carving midair
left hand still closed
        in sleep

    & this time i trace
    the medial version
who   like us   is touched
    by what comes before
& after

i ride the curves cool & smooth
    as a line of breath   though i can't see
the whole page   i still listen for the story
    my ش wanted to tell:

shukr rising   thanks be to all
who rowed this pencil-boat before us

& all who offered us their oars

(ii) *qaf*

Inside the night a shawl gathers
at my throat where shyness lives.

I flick the tail of the ق with my tongue
& the word قلم rises, pencil I swallowed

who tilts my chin to the moon: القمر
I repeat, holding her meat half-formed

& shining in the maroon sky of my mouth.
I worry I've been deprived of a mother-

tongue but am wrong. القمر is a gift lifted
by the needleworker who practices behind

my curtain of teeth, spinning new muscle
& sinew. I heave my ق into cool air thick

with cloth pockets of speech. I feel for
the seams, for the sounds trying to be.

IV.

The only language of loss left in the world is Arabic—

—Agha Shahid Ali

parable of the aleph

ا

aleph, arrow, sapling, wand

needle that lengthens what comes before

ink stroke who draws sound
& bears the little hamza

    see:

    girl squatting at the base of a tree إ

        or

    girl perched atop a stone pillar أ

studying
  the thousand ruins

      ألف ألف ألف

parable of the three sisters

(i)

ب

studying the thousand ruins
girl sees ox horns, belly,
boat who ferries to & fro

&: smallest scale weighing desire:

    (i want)   بدي

    (tomorrow)   بكرا

    (dad)   بابا

    (i love)   بحب

    (house)   بيت

    (girl, daughter)   بنت

    (enough)   بس

iwanttomorrowdadilovehousegirldaughterenoughenoughdaughter
   girlhouseilovedadtomorrowiwant

i love dad
i love house
i love girldaughter
i love tomorrow
i love enough

        girl i love

(ii)

ت

girl loves to touch
a teacup to her tulips
to try the saucer
as tinkling bell
to turn the cup
upside down
to tip it as a hat
to trace the shape
of her big sister
grinning
to lift her like a tray
    of crystal & twirl
teeth flashing

maybe girl's sister
is laughing

ta-ta-ta-ta-ta-ta-ta-ta-ta

(iii)

ث

girl's father fills a bowl
    with fresh mulberries.

see it? in Arabic we say
    nus-nus. meaning half

for you & half for me.
    our teeth speckled

with purple seeds. girl sees
    ox grazing in the bottom

of the bowl. crow flocks
    his horns. girl makes

her tongue a slab of meat
    between rows of teeth.

th! th! th! : sound of feet
    slicing through snow.

parable of the three cousins

(i)

ح

girl is the little essence
her one eye who never blinks

she is the dark part
heart's center

        innermost kernel

    umbilicus
        aureole

            fish
            darting

Eye of Horus
    & good health

falcon's eye in flight
    eye of the camel's

slow hump
tipping   girl back
    to earth

(ii)

ح

girl fogs a mirror
        in the mouth of sea

puffs out her lungs to match
        sparrow's breast,

skirt swishing breathy
        in the courtyard.

She touches ح like a door
        knocker, gust of air

sweeping in, sail hauled up,
        raspy wave cresting.

girl's mother coos *babybear*
        over the phone

        &
        حياتي

(iii)

خ

girl skates down the alley
    legs loose & arms wide

        black dress billowing

she tears a crust
    of bread & chews

        while dead leaves
rustle under the neighbor's rake—

  akhh, akhh, akhh

parable of broken bones

(i)

د

door
(d)ear
as in dad
bell; crook
of girl's arm
fractured
bone

(ii)

ذ

girl leans forward, clasps her cast close. she draws cats and tulips on the plaster that holds her arm in place. she faces west & folds over her legs, worry making of her spine a sloping hill, the rocks loose & tumbling.
   when her friend Four Hornets lands nearby, they make rhymes together: *swarm* rhymes with *mourn*. *torch* rhymes with *search*. *alone* with *grown*.
      girl lists words she loves for Four Hornets: *hooves, hum, rib, oil*. Four Hornets listens—*lantern, apricot, wood*—*by the way, serendipity* ! then it's Four Hornets' turn: Four Hornets pierces words into girl's calves, each one leaving a welt. the air vibrates in girl's ear,

dhhhh, dhhhhh, dhhhhh, dhhhhhhh

parable of the field

(i)   ⊃ *girl practices reading in both directions*

oh busted knuckle	busted knuckle oh
oh rusted scalpel	rusted scalpel oh
oh radish tail	radish pale oh
& fingernail	fingernail &
oh crescent moon	crescent moon
oh comma	oh comma
oh shoulder bone	shoulder bone
& wheezing lung	wheezing lung &
oh ghost sailing	oh ghost sailing
beneath the eyelid	beneath eyelid
stitched with sleep	with stitched sleep
oh brushstroke	oh brushstrokes
& teeny muffler	teeny & mufflers
oh ant-sized scarf	sized-ant oh scarves
& wish blown lash	wish blown lash &
they say you come	you say come
from the pictogram	from pictogram
of a head, they call	call they ahead
you *alveolar uvular*	*alveolar uvular* you
& *liquid consonant*	& *liquid consonant*
which means slippery	which means slippery
when clustered	clustered when
but I love to slip	I but love to slip
on you little thrill,	you little on
trickling creek,	thrill trickling
tap shoe, you	creek tap shoe
are the puff	are you puff
pastry of rolled	pastry of rolled
up r, the ruffled	& r ruffled
rose & snail, your	rose & snail
speech is a snare	speech a ensnare
drum, oh flutter	drum oh flutter
& fern curled	ferned & curled

in the moss,
leaf skipping
across a field
of flax, you
canter & break
into gallop,
wind trilling
under your
horse hoof—

the in moss,
leaf skipping
a across field
flax of you
canter & break
into gallop
wind trilling
under your
—hoarse & hoof

(ii)

ز

Girl finds a human shape

      lilting soul

           angel in flight

Here is her candle

      & wick

           newly lit

Here is her scythe

      listen as she combs

           the grasses

      zza

           zza

                zza !

parable of thanks

(i)

س

sea
stitch
sun
(wheel-
barrow)
sack
silver-
spoon
susurrus
sister
see

(ii)

ش

the shape of the sheen is said to mimic
the structure of the human heart:

lower larger left ventricle supplies the full body
smaller right ventricle supplies the lungs

                                                            ^   three
                                         ^   small tufts
                shukr rises up ^

parable of sound & grammar

(i)

ص

here is your oldest sound

may you undo the laces of your tongue
& fill like a kite, floating skyward

       is this your ribbon?
       your half-knot?

          (half not?)

may your wing grow long with this sound
may it be a spoon you lift to your mouth

may you release the sharpened hook
of shame & throw your body back,

               fish, girl, swim.

(ii)

ض

The pharynx or epiglottis is constricted during the articulation of this sound. The epiglottis is a flap of cartilage at the root of the tongue, which is depressed during swallowing to cover the opening of the windpipe. The epiglottis is leaf-shaped.

This letter is called the ḍād. In English, this spelling resembles the word *dad,* as in father. But in fact *dad* with a short *a* (*sad* or *bad*) is not the correct sound value here. The actual sound value is deep and thick. It is a long ancient sound that comes from the root. The closest way I could write the sound in English is: *ddaawhdd.* The tongue curls almost as if to make an *l* shape, I think.

In my careful search I have learned that Arabic, the language of my mother's people, and the adopted language of my father, is sometimes referred to as "the language of the ḍād" (لغة الضاد). It is said that this particular sound value is considered to be the direct ancestor of Arabic ḍād merging with the ṣād.

    I see: ancestor of dad merging with sad.

    Girl sees: fish, bubble, footprint, bunny, bucket, person filling basket

                                with tongue-shaped leaves.

parable of sharing

(i)

ط

girl brings a ladle
to dole out soup

she sets the table
with Four Hornets

together they eat

(ii)

ظ

bird drinking or

half butterfly or

girl planting sapling or

girl touching her toes or

girl leaning against tree or

girl holding tree or

tree holding girl

parable of the eye in the throat

(i)

ع

    innermost letter   to emerge from the throat   & scraped up gut

        ancestor to the letter O
                O of circumference
                O of looking eye to eye
                O of utterance: lips a round
                              puff of breath

Al-Khalil ibn Ahmad al-Farahidi, writer of the first Arabic dictionary in the 8th century, suggests that the ع (ʿayn) is the first sound, the essential sound, both the voice and a representation of the self

> *I am the name of the sound*
>   *and the sound of the name.*
> *I am the sign of the letter*
>   *and the designation of the division*[1]

    my difficulty gathering a strong ع troubles my sense of self

        عيوني

    (girl says: I'd give my eyes for you)

---

[1] "Thunder, Perfect Mind," *The Nag Hammadi*. Also known as the Gnostic Gospels, *The Nag Hammadi* is a collection of early Christian and Gnostic texts. Thirteen leather-bound papyrus manuscripts that date back to the 3rd and 4th centuries were found buried in a sealed jar near the Egyptian town of Nag Hammadi in 1945.

(ii)

غ

in the morning
girl hears Fairuz singing

أعطني الناي وغني

parable as ars poetica

(i)

ف

The shape of the *Fā'* is assumed to come from a pictogram of the mouth. Girl sees a curled shoe, a buckle or person sitting with legs outstretched & toes flexed, arms making a pleasing loop, head studying something small.

Girl rests her oars in the oarlocks & takes notes:

> *Fā'-fathah* (فَ / fa) is a multifunction prefix equivalent to "so" or "so that"
>
> Example: نَكْتُب *naktub* means *we write*
>
> ف + نَكْتُب → فَنَكْتُب *fanaktub* means *so we write*

(ii)

ق

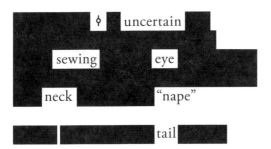

(iii)

ك

1. كف *Kaff* (palm; palm of a hand)

2. In literary Arabic, ك (*ka*) is used as a particle to mean *like* or *as*

3. If *kaff* is the palm of a hand and *ka* means *like* or *as*, then maybe this brings us to simile

4. Simile: a hand touching two places at once; a hand bringing together two faraway things, making a transfer (metaphor)

5. For example:

    كَطَائِر (*like a bird* or *as though a bird*)

6. **poem**

    girl
    as though
    a bird
    hand

parable of water & mothers

(i)

ل

girl draws her bucket
up from the well

her mother calls تعالي
finger beckoning *come home*

mother like a shepherd
with her pastoral staff

pastoral like a swan
circling in the ripple

(ii)

م

girl's favorite shape
is the meem. she loves
to make it with her
asthoughabirdhand

         م   م   م   م

        curdled milk   curl of soul
snake rearing   sharp nose

   ميم ميم   ميم   ميم   ميم

مممممممممممممممstroke cruelمممممممم
& sweetممممممممممممممممmeemممممم
cameممممممممfrom a symbolمممممم
ممممم ممممممم ممممممfor waterممhence
the words mayyمممممmaiممممممma
ممممممممممممممmamaممممممم
مممممممممممممممم*immee*ممممممم

(iii)

ن

Girl's favorite word is نحن

It means *We*

Even before she knew the word she loved the sound

Here: *Nahnou*

Maybe she loves it because it sounds like ننون

Or maybe because Girl is thinking about We

Girl wonders areyoumyWe?

AmIyourWe?

HowdoWeWetogether?

WouldyouWewithme?

CouldIWewithyou?

HowcanIbetterWeyou?

&YouMe? AndusWe?

In Arabic, there is an expression:

"nus-nus" (remember?)

It means half-half

Half for you & half for me

ForWe

parable of the monostich

(i)

هـ girl, snail glistering forward

(ii)

و girl, softcry, from

(iii)

ي girl, bird   flown

V.

Arab American Syntax

I touch the peachgold petals of a rose in my friend's garden. We are visiting her in Maine. It is Tuesday, August 4, 2020. The wind damp & close.

In the afternoon my loved one texts me: *I don't want to live in this world.*

She sends photos of her friends' apartments, furniture showered with glass. In the living room a chandelier lies in a heap on the floor, a giant spider whose legs have collapsed around the body, light extinguished. Rebar hangs like stalactites from the ceiling.

> Experiment:
>
> When there's no ceiling left, how do we assemble the sentence? Do we say *rebar hanging like stalactites from no ceiling*? Or, *rebar hanging like stalactites from the ceiling that is no longer there*?
>
> The word *ceiling* implies presence. What is the syntax for absence? Disaster? How does the shattered sentence say?

In one photo a friend cries & clutches her cheeks, eyebrows arched as though straining to stay attached to her face. A channel of blood runs from her hairline to her chin.

In another: a crumbling stairwell, a hospital room turned inside out. The bed empty, save a single clay-red stain on the pillow.

Hooves trot up & down the slopes of my chest. A pool of water lapping at my navel: desperate gratitude that my loved one was not in Beirut when the hangar blew. The water ripples each time I remember.

I touch my knees & draw them inward like gathering my children in my arms. Not knowing how to pray in Arabic, not having children to gather, I tap my fingers against my clavicles. A drum I make to accompany the clatter of horses.

> Relationship: Long Distance
>
> I am not there, I am here. Here: on the sunken blue couch in a house, intact. The coordinates of my *I* & *eye* are charted with distance.
>
> Distance is my luck & my long grief.

My loved one left Beirut after eight years. She loved the city even as it ate its way through her, hollowing her body from inside like the hornworm who burrows into the tomato, drilling a small perfect hole with its teeth.

When I say the city tore through her, I mean she came back a packet of bone & wing.

What she left behind: a turtle who still lives on the balcony, slowly chewing through lettuce leaves. A swirling mural she painted in yellows on the side of her apartment. Half her tongue. Her quick footsteps that kissed the night streets.

Residues flicker in my mind. The *clip-clop-clip-clop* of high-heeled shoes down a sleek hallway. Imprints of fingers along doorknobs & walls. Ink blots & paper stained with spilled tea, flecks of saliva, breadcrumbs. The worn-in soles of slippers.

It's been six years since I walked barefoot along the Mediterranean, retracing my parents' footsteps, touching the very same sidewalks as my uncles & grandparents & great aunts & cousins.

I wonder if the arches of my loved one's feet still rest somewhere in the sand, untouched by the blast. I imagine Hamra's folded ears listening for the song of my loved one's heels.

*

I realize I've avoided calling myself Lebanese because
of a problem with syntax.

So much is left out of the sentence however I arrange the words.

People raise their eyebrows, ask for proof.

If I was born, grew up, have family there. If I'm Muslim.
If I speak Lebanese.

If where you are from corresponds to where you were born,
here are my sentences:

I was born in Nicosia, Cyprus on May 18, 1990.

I remember the smell of tahinopita & a pair of long fluorescent
lights on the kitchen ceiling.

What I know is the feeling of things. When I say *Cyprus*
it feels like terracotta pots filled with sesame & honey.

A tongue rolled up like the spire of a snail.

Wind trilling through each whorl. Weight of warm bread
in my hand.

My lips make a pretty shape for *Nicosia*. I nearly sing the word,
a string of minor notes.

Four syllables that twinkle blue in my ear, kingdom of warbling
sea.

For years I carried an eraser that was shaped like Cyprus
with a map of the island printed on its surface in primary colors.
Probably a trinket from a gift shop.

I loved to hold it in my hand like a soft hook, touching
& smelling the sharp sweet rubber on my fingers.

I lost the eraser somewhere along the way
to America.

Is where you come from what you have lost along the way?

*

Maybe it's an exercise in arithmetic:

    mom + dad
    +/- American grandparents who lived in Lebanon
    +/- Helly & Vladimir (Helly who died long before)
    +/- 2 Khalos who left Beirut during the war(s)
    +/- mom's extended family in Buenos Aires
    - when we moved to America from Pakistan, not Lebanon
    + rolling waraq enab at home, a pinky width of filling
      in each wet leaf
    - speaking English
    + visiting my loved one in Beirut
    _____

    = one cephalopod who inches up & down
      my throat, weeping their shiny fluid

*

H leaves a voice memo saying his brother just bought

a flat near our old house, in case Beirut collapses completely.

*

For the eight years that my loved one lived in Beirut

I couldn't bring myself to go except once to visit

while she moved apartments, after a breakup.

All those years I told myself time, money, health.

Had I not lived so far from Lebanon for so long,

I would have gone.

*

On the phone my mother shares that my loved one

is angry about our trip to Lebanon. She has told

my mother *you can't go to Lebanon. Lebanon is mine.*

*

I wonder what it means to be Lebanese.

I see footage of the blast and look away. I stay. I play & replay.

I scrape together a response when people check in,
asking if I'm okay.

Hey, I heard about what happened in Beirut. Are you okay? Is your family okay?

I assemble a sentence with the right parts: subject-verb-predicate.

We are okay. Sometimes: *it's awful, it's so sad. We're fine, hamdulillah. It's terrible what's happened.*

I swallow what is absent from the sentence. Have I been absent from you, Lebanon?

Have you been absent from me? I look at family photos, studying shyly the script on street signs I cannot write or read.

I practice my syllables & my glottal stops.

I greet the cat: *Marhaba ya Tantoun.* I see my Sitto's crowded teeth as she pulls open the sliding door,

calling to us, almost singing *ahlan wa sahlan.*

Notes

Invocation

Refers to the common Arabic household word "zankha" (زنخة) which is often used to describe the eggy/redolent smell associated with poultry and eggs.

Heritage Language

Sukuun means "silence." It is a pronunciation marker (ْ) used to indicate the absence of a vowel following the consonant above which it is written.

Origin Story

The quote by Mahmoud Darwish appears in a collection of interviews called *Mahmoud Darwish: Palestine as Metaphor*, translated by Amira El-Zein and Carolyn Forché.

"a phoenix appears / in love with living / who, for the sake / of a new beginning / will burn itself alive" borrows language from the poem "Resurrection and Ashes" by Adonis.

When I Wake

Refers to and borrows language from the poem "I wake and feel the fell of dark, not day" by Gerard Manley Hopkins.

Dream, or Poem to the Tongue

The poem's final line refers to the Arabic expression تقبريني or, 'may you bury me,' expressing a wish that the loved one outlive the speaker.

On Sisterhood

This poem is written after Lucille Clifton's poem, "cruelty. don't talk to me about cruelty."

Learning to Write in Arabic

قلم means "pencil"

القمر means "the moon"

parable of the aleph

ألف *'alf* is Arabic for "one thousand."

parable of the three cousins

حياتي "Hayati" is a term of endearment used for loved ones, meaning 'my life.'

parable of the eye in the throat

Fairuz, sometimes referred to as "the soul of Lebanon" is the Arab world's reigning songstress.

أعطني الناي وغني (Give me the Flute and Sing) is a beloved song sung by many, including Fairuz. The song is based on a poem by Lebanese poet Khalil Gibran.

parable of the monostich

A monostich is a poem which consists of a single line. This final parable is a reference to "The Lost Son," in which Theodore Roethke writes:

Snail, snail glister me forward, / Bird soft-sigh me home, / Worm be with me. / This is my hard time.

Arab American Syntax

The final Arabic expression here, "ahlan wa sahlan," literally means "welcome" but is used commonly in the Arab world like the English "hello." It is a shortening of the original:

حَلَلْتَ أهلاً ونزَلتَ سهلاً

halalta ahlan wa nazalta sahlan

halalta - "you have come/arrived"

ahlan - accusative form of *ahl* which means family. You can say *ahli* to mean, "my parents & siblings" and also to mean, "my people."

nazalta - "to come down, descend, or stay in a place or someone's house." From that we also have the word *manzil* for "house."

sahlan - accusative form of *sahl* which means "plain or easy land/road."

The full translation is: you have come to a people who are like kinsfolk/family, and to a place that is smooth/plain/easy, or not rugged.

The phrase was later shortened to *ahlan wa sahlan*.

Acknowledgments

Thank you to the editors of the following publications, for offering a home to these poems, sometimes in earlier forms:

The Adroit Journal: "How the Dream Ends";
Beloit Poetry Journal: "On Form & Matter," "Just Had to Tell Somebody," "Origin Story," "Heritage Language";
Gulf Coast: "Arab American Syntax";
Michigan Quarterly Review Online: "Transit";
Mizna: "Strays";
Ninth Letter: "Requiem For the Blue-Headed Morning";
River Styx: "Now that You're Gone";
The Rumpus: "*parable as ars poetica*," "*parable of water & mothers*," "Invocation," "Return (the retelling)," "Return (the etymologies)," "Return (the wish)."

*

The thing about acknowledgements is that they are, it seems to me, possibly never ending. Wherever to begin? And more worrisome still, where, and when (oh, how!) to conclude? It's no joke when I say this thanks is bottomless. Is an entire book. Coincidentally, one's first book might occasion an especially thorough, studied catalogue of influence and support, because the object here is the result of years of labor & dreaming & touch coming to life for the first time. This *labordreamingtouch* belonging to many more than myself: alive and dead, human and mineral, seen and subterranean.

& so: I kneel to the elders, teachers, students (who teach me, who challenge me!), friends, sycamores, city benches, poppy fields, alley cats, dirt, books, birdtalk, waterways, and light who make my writing and my life possible. This work is also yours.

A great gasp of gratitude to Aracelis Girmay for saying what if? And to Peter for saying yes. So much thanks to Justine, Sandy, Benjamin, Isabella—the whole team at BOA. Without you there is no book!

To Mr. Bill Jones, my high school Creative Writing teacher, who watered the teenage seeds of my poetry with the genius of Lucille Clifton and Naomi Shihab Nye, Sandra Cisneros and Mary Oliver. How lucky. How lifesaving, in fact. Thank you, wherever you are.

Lifelong affection to Ellen Doré Watson, Joan Larkin, and Annie Boutelle, who are among my poetry aunties and who showed me early on what a life in poems might be: lush, pleasurable, raucous with dissent and good company.

To Kevin Quashie, who once said to me, maybe in Stoddard Hall: *you are alive.* Thank you for this foundation. Your teachings and attention changed my life, change my life, rearrange me.

All my م to Carolina Ebeid, for the tributaries we share. I carry your work(I carry your work inside my work)since the Bucknell Seminar days. Thank you for the song that you are.

Which, see how thanks begets thanks? Armfuls to Jeffrey Pethybridge, for offering generous counsel, encouragement, and solidarity from inside the joint ruins of capitalism and empire.

To Nathalie Handal and Donia Salem Harhoor, thank you for your midwifery and mentorship (tysm RAWI!). Donia: your heart which is medicine. Nathalie: your dreamy imagination, for moving the book toward Arabic.

Aracelis again & again—(d)earest, pleated accordions of thanks, my eternal singing. Thank you for opening the door wide and welcoming me through. I am always writing with and toward you, my language deepening to touch yours.

Bobbi Bigs, o! Praise this giant wheelbarrow of debt, which I'll be wheeling around forever, weeping & laughing at once. If trees, these poems grow into & out of your shade & branch. And if okra flowers, well, all the okra flowers in my heart speak your name. Thank you.

*

In addition to the above dear & luminous, I'm grateful for support from the Stadler Center, Vermont Studio Center, Fine Arts Work Center, and MFA program at Indiana University, which have provided immeasurable gifts of time, space, and community. Great gratitude too for the Fulbright grant that allowed me to return to Cyprus & Lebanon to work on this book.

Speaking of! Gros bisous to the Mroue/El Bacha crew for taking us in and bringing the music; Diyala, Joumana, Joyce, Shazi, Xaritsa, Eleni, et al, for being family thirty years later; bougainvilleas of thanks to Lisa Suhair Majaj for your strong, wise poems and light. To Nadya Sbaiti and Rima Rantisi: for sharing your love of Beirut with me, as well as fortifying me with advice and support.

Extra special soul singing to Mahita & Fatima, for your generous collaboration on the artwork for this book's cover. Thank you for sharing your father's beautiful work with me. May these poems also honor his legacy.

*

The bones of this book formed while I was a graduate student in Bloomington, Indiana, and I'm grateful to so many folks who helped me create a home (thank you, Wendy!) in the Midwest.

Adrian, thanks for encouraging me to take the Fulbright—what a lucky year of writing and research. Big hugs to Romayne, for your kindness and generosity, in both literary endeavors and transcontinental moves. Thank you, Stacey, for fanning out my poems on the long table at Soma and helping me see the connective tissue. Merci, Bill, for homemade pesto, monarch butterflies, and conversations about writing in your garden. Quel bonheur!

To the many other teachers and guides at Indiana University, and to the visiting artists who came through and sprinkled their fairy dust over us—a well of gratitude. The sweetest pawpaws and persimmons go to my IUMFA peers, especially Austin, Alberto, L., Alex, Hannah, WLS, Sully, Essence, Anni, Gionni, Soleil,

Meredith, Noah, Saami, El, Rose, and Laura. As well as to the marvelous folks in the wider Bloomington community with whom I've been so fortunate to share space.

So many poets have offered guidance, care, and little sparks of madness where our paths have touched: Jean Valentine, Jamaal May, Dan Beachy-Quick, GC Waldrep, Javier Zamora, Christopher Citro, Samantha Tetangco, Kaveh Akbar, Tracy Fuad, Noah Baldino, and plenty more. Thank you.

*

Circles and circles of we—

To friends and family scattered in time and place, without whom I would not be: my sweet Sitto, memory eternal; my parents (mama: all my writing is meant to please you, thank you for teaching me that language is a matter of life and death; my bright and tender baba/dad/MKS; my sister, Yusra, with whom I learn the length of love. My constellations of kin, all who have supported my work and who I name in my body as my lifelines. I kiss the ground. I work to honor you:

KK (MEOWMIX), RYAN (MY FRIEND!), AMANDA, MAI, EMILY, LILLY (ABLETELL), OLLIE, SAAMI (SHMOOPY; RIVERSOF), BAB, ALBERTO, DIMA, JORDAN, JOJO, KAYLA, MAU, BOO, D, BAMBI, ANNA (أنا), AL (RIP) &

Logan, whatever a sun will always sing is you—

& Nancy, seriously—for deeper support.

And you! Mighty reader, thank you for peering into these pages with me.

I'm saying, in my particular, long (could be longer!) way: I've been accompanied at every stage. May I return this gift always, and all ways.

*

This book is dedicated to the memory of Dr. Zaineb Istrabadi (1955-2021), allah yerhamha, and her five cats, whom she dearly loved: Pasha, Czarina, Filfil, Mishmish, and Buddy.

About the Author

janan alexandra is the daughter of a Lebanese mother and a Beirut-born American father. Her life has been peripatetic, with roots scattered in Cyprus, Lebanon, Pakistan, England, France, and many corners of North America. Since 2015, janan has taught poetry and creative writing in schools, libraries, youth arts centers, Zoom Rooms, and carceral spaces. Along with language work, janan has facilitated restorative movement classes; nannied for families; welded ice cream scoops; tied oyster nets; tended land and animals; built furniture; baked bread; painted houses; and busked fiddle tunes to make a living. She is the third generation in her family to bow her head to the people of Palestine and stand in solidarity with their struggle for liberation and self-determination. At the time of writing this, we are entering the 13th month of the Gaza Genocide, the latest catastrophe in 75+ years of ongoing colonial violence. janan urges you to join the interconnected movements for life, freedom, and justice everywhere, in whatever ways you can. May poetry be a place where we hold history accountable to language and activate our deepest political commitments, our most revolutionary love.

BOA Editions, Ltd. A. Poulin, Jr. New Poets of America Series

No. 1 *Cedarhome*
Poems by Barton Sutter
Foreword by W. D. Snodgrass

No. 2 *Beast Is a Wolf with Brown Fire*
Poems by Barry Wallenstein
Foreword by M. L. Rosenthal

No. 3 *Along the Dark Shore*
Poems by Edward Byrne
Foreword by John Ashbery

No. 4 *Anchor Dragging*
Poems by Anthony Piccione
Foreword by Archibald MacLeish

No. 5 *Eggs in the Lake*
Poems by Daniela Gioseffi
Foreword by John Logan

No. 6 *Moving the House*
Poems by Ingrid Wendt
Foreword by William Stafford

No. 7 *Whomp and Moonshiver*
Poems by Thomas Whitbread
Foreword by Richard Wilbur

No. 8 *Where We Live*
Poems by Peter Makuck
Foreword by Louis Simpson

No. 9 *Rose*
Poems by Li-Young Lee
Foreword by Gerald Stern

No. 10 *Genesis*
Poems by Emanuel di Pasquale
Foreword by X. J. Kennedy

No. 11 *Borders*
Poems by Mary Crow
Foreword by David Ignatow

No. 12 *Awake*
Poems by Dorianne Laux
Foreword by Philip Levine

No. 13 *Hurricane Walk*
Poems by Diann Blakely Shoaf
Foreword by William Matthews

No. 14 *The Philosopher's Club*
Poems by Kim Addonizio
Foreword by Gerald Stern

No. 15 *Bell 8*
Poems by Rick Lyon
Foreword by C. K. Williams

No. 16 *Bruise Theory*
Poems by Natalie Kenvin
Foreword by Carolyn Forché

No. 17 *Shattering Air*
Poems by David Biespiel
Foreword by Stanley Plumly

No. 18 *The Hour Between Dog and Wolf*
Poems by Laure-Anne Bosselaar
Foreword by Charles Simic

No. 19 *News of Home*
Poems by Debra Kang Dean
Foreword by Colette Inez

No. 20 *Meteorology*
Poems by Alpay Ulku
Foreword by Yusef Komunyakaa

No. 21 *The Daughters of Discordia*
Poems by Suzanne Owens
Foreword by Denise Duhamel

No. 22 *Rare Earths*
Poems by Deena Linett
Foreword by Molly Peacock

No. 23 *An Unkindness of Ravens*
        Poems by Meg Kearney
        Foreword by Donald Hall

No. 24 *Hunting Down the Monk*
        Poems by Adrie Kusserow
        Foreword by Karen Swenson

No. 25 *Big Back Yard*
        Poems by Michael Teig
        Foreword by Stephen Dobyns

No. 26 *Elegy with a Glass of Whiskey*
        Poems by Crystal Bacon
        Foreword by Stephen Dunn

No. 27 *The Eclipses*
        Poems by David Woo
        Selected by Michael S. Harper

No. 28 *Falling to Earth*
        Poems by Tom Hansen
        Foreword by Molly Peacock

No. 29 *Even the Hollow My Body Made Is Gone*
        Poems by Janice N. Harrington
        Foreword by Elizabeth Spires

No. 30 *The Boatloads*
        Poems by Dan Albergotti
        Foreword by Edward Hirsch

No. 31 *Awayward*
        Poems by Jennifer Kronovet
        Foreword by Jean Valentine

No. 32 *Beautiful in the Mouth*
        Poems by Keetje Kuipers
        Foreword by Thomas Lux

No. 33 *Walking the Dog's Shadow*
        Poems by Deborah Brown
        Foreword by Tony Hoagland

No. 34 *Litany for the City*
        Poems by Ryan Teitman
        Foreword by Jane Hirshfield

No. 35 *The Stick Soldiers*
        Poems by Hugh Martin
        Foreword by Cornelius Eady

No. 36 *Revising the Storm*
        Poems by Geffrey Davis
        Foreword by Dorianne Laux

No. 37 *Shame | Shame*
        Poems by Devin Becker
        Foreword by David St. John

No. 38 *Trouble the Water*
        Poems by Derrick Austin
        Foreword by Mary Szybist

No. 39 *When I Grow Up I Want to Be a List of Further Possibilities*
        Poems by Chen Chen
        Foreword by Jericho Brown

No. 40 *Cenzontle*
        Poems by Marcelo Hernandez Castillo
        Foreword by Brenda Shaughnessy

No. 41 *Rail*
        Poems by Kai Carlson-Wee
        Foreword by Nick Flynn

No. 42 *Documents*
        Poems by Jan-Henry Gray
        Foreword by D. A. Powell

No. 43 *Tracing the Horse*
        Poems by Diana Marie Delgado
        Foreword by Luis J. Rodriguez

No. 44 *Improvisation Without Accompaniment*
        Poems by Matt Morton
        Foreword by Patricia Smith

No. 45 *How to Be Better by Being Worse*
        Poems by Justin Jannise
        Foreword by Richard Blanco

No. 46 *Two Brown Dots*
        Poems by Danni Quintos
        Foreword by Aimee Nezhukumatathil

No. 47 *Casual Conversation*
       Poems by Renia White
       Foreword by Aracelis Girmay
No. 48 *A Shiver in the Leaves*
       Poems by Luther Hughes
       Foreword by Carl Phillips
No. 49 *Good Grief, the Ground*
       Poems by Margaret Ray
       Foreword by Stephanie Burt
No. 50 *fox woman get out!*
       Poems by India Lena
       González
       Foreword by Aracelis Girmay
No. 51 *Conversation Among Stones*
       Poems by Willie Lin
No. 52 *Beforelight*
       Poems by Matthew Gellman
       Foreword by Tina Chang
No. 53 *d-sorientation*
       Poems by Charleen McClure
       Foreword by Aracelis Girmay
No. 54 *Sons of Salt*
       Poems by Yaccaira Salvatierra
No. 55 *Second Nature*
       Poems by Chaun Ballard
       Foreword by Matthew
       Shenoda
No. 56 *come from*
       Poems by janan alexandra
       Foreword by Ross Gay

Colophon

BOA Editions, Ltd., a not-for-profit publisher of poetry and other literary works, fosters readership and appreciation of contemporary literature. By identifying, cultivating, and publishing both new and established poets and selecting authors of unique literary talent, BOA brings high-quality literature to the public.

Support for this effort comes from the sale of its publications, grant funding, and private donations.

*

The publication of this book is made possible, in part, by the special support of the following individuals:

Anonymous (x2)
Angela Bonazinga & Catherine Lewis
Ralph Black & Susan Murphy
Mark Cuddy & Christina Selian
Chris Dahl, *in honor of Chuck Hertrick*
Bonnie Garner
James Hale
Kelly Hatton
Peg Heminway
Nora A. Jones
Joe & Dale Klein
Barbara Lovenheim, *in memory of John Lovenheim*
Joe McElveney
Boo Poulin, *in memory of A. Poulin Jr.*
Deborah Ronnen
John H. Schultz
William Waddell & Linda Rubel
Michael Waters & Mihaela Moscaliuc